struggle and challenges mothers face

Table of contents

Chapter 1: Single and Young Mothers

Single Mothers

Raising a child is a grueling experience. It's indeed more grueling for a single Mother . We see a growing number of problems single mothers face in society: fiscal struggles, lack of support, emotional battles, consummations and numerous further. The struggles of being a single Mother can hit you enough wretchedly. So, what can you do to manage the problems single Mothersface in society?

exploration onU.S. mothers shows that among wedded mothers(68), a sizable percent(24) are single mothers. The number of children living with a single parent is growing fleetly around the globe. Being a single parent can be relatively stressful, both for the parent and the child. Beyond that, the moment's parent faces unique

parenthood challenges, the rise of digital media, bullying, and high- stakes testing in early childhood. So, in this composition, I've listed some common problems single mothers
 face in society along with some suggestions to help you deal with them.

1. Work- Life Challenges
Parenthood has Norway been harder. According to a Pew check, fifty- nine percent of full- time working mothers
 say they do n't have enough rest time. It's indeed harder to balance work and parenthood for single working mothers. A single Mother is supposed to take care of the kiddies and give for them all by herself. To be suitable to give for the children she frequently has no choice but to put in redundant working hours. thus, balancing the professional liabilities and parenthood is a major problem faced by single mothers

2. Guilt, condemn, and Responsibility
 utmost single mothers

are hugely sick of the fatherhood and guilt rhetoric — especially working single Mother . They frequently feel like they 're even coming up suddenly when it comes to doing enough for their kiddies. Not to mention their master and extended family, and yes, of course, their community. As single mothers, they've to do all of these things alone, and it's not always easy.

Suggestions for Single mothers The good news is that with right strategies you can overcome Mother guilt and get the other delicate feelings under control.

Accept that parenthood is not a competition and there's no right or wrong way to parent.
Limit your social media operation.
Learn to live in the moment.
Spend quality time with your kiddies.
Take time for yourself.
Connect with like- inclined mothers.

3. Emotional Challenges

Being a single Mother means that there's no bone
there to partake the good and bad guests . She does n't have anyone to look at her favorite pictures with when she ca n't find a sitter. She keeps on juggling between professional and particular lives. As a result, the sense of loneliness and depression starts to creep in.

Suggestions for Single Mothers In these turbulent times, you have to be flexible. Focus on the positive side of solo parenthood and-

produce a healthy and loving terrain for your sprat.

Be thankful that you're suitable to give on your own.

Find others to serve as part models.

Educate them to play sports or dig for worms or whatever they like to do.

Remind yourself that no bone
is perfect, and you're doing great because your spirit is happy and thriving.

4. fiscal Strain

Lack of fiscal support is a reality for numerous single mothers. While it's true that " plutocrats ca n't buy happiness ", a lack of plutocrats can beget stress, anxiety and limited choices. Single mothers are more likely to feel shamefaced of not furnishing enough for the kiddies. The situation aggravates when they're left staying for child support that nowadays arrives, or they've to pay attorneys to pursue what should be paid.

Suggestions for Single mothers Then are the five keys to fiscal success for single mothers

Come economical.
Determine what you owe.
Find a plutocrat to pay down debt.
Use a yearly budget template to track charges.
Save for the short- and long- term.

5. Limited Time and Fatigue

The hardest part of being a single Mother is prioritizing time and concentrating on tone- care. utmost single working mothers

feel exhausted trying to hold down jobs and insure their children attend extra-curricular conditioning. The very act of taking care of a baby and work liabilities can be draining in numerous situations — emotionally, cognitively, and psychologically.

Suggestions for Single mothers First understand that taking care of yourself is important.However, you can not take care of others, If you do n't take care of yourself. So, how can you recharge your batteries? Take a quick look at these easy energy boosters for ideas!

Eat further red meat and keep protein-rich snacks while on the go – similar as nuts, rubbish, and crackers or an energy ball.
Drink tons of water to keep energy situations high and feel fresh from daylight to evening.

Drink a glass of herbal tea or bomb water in the morning, keep a bottle of water in the handbag or auto and insure you drink whenever you have a mess.

Spend lower time on the phone.

Take small rest breaks during the day.

Find time for exercise by incorporating fitness into everyday routines, similar as kiddies play-dates or taking the little bones

to the academy.

rather than lying down while the kiddies play in the rumpus room, take them for a long walk to the demesne rather.

Despite all of this, single mothers frequently admit review in moment's society. Being a single parent takes lots of courage, practice taking deep breaths for many twinkles when you lose your tolerance.

young mother

Difficulties young mother's Face Each Day

The lives of new mothers can be incredibly grueling . Millions of women are facing analogous issues with their first babies.

Some of the biggest problems are constant privation of sleep and, therefore, fatigue, hard recovery, and pain, everyday stress, or indeed depression. To complicate matters, Young mothers
 suffer the most because of the lack of " me " time and ferocious schedule.
These common issues prove that fatherhood, and especially its first times, is a real challenge by itself. still, pupil- mothers face indeed more difficulties.

The number of women carrying a university degree has been snowballing for decades; the number of pupil mothers
 was growing as well. In common sense, Young mothers
 are no longer considered " traditional " scholars. Unlike their peers, they witness a briskly

transition into majority touched off not by council, but by domestic responsibility.

Top Biggest Challenges Young Mothers Face

Trying to perform binary places, council scholars who are formerly raising their children can stumble upon a wide range of difficulties. Getting used to the massive responsibility of fatherhood can be hard. Still, this thrilling time of your life does n't inescapably have to be dulled with lots of problems!

Being well apprehensive of the forthcoming challenges and possible results, one may be completely fortified! To help Young mothers make a smoother transition into a new part, we've prepared a list of the top five most significant difficulties and results that can help overcome them!

Studying

Studying is delicate and time- consuming by itself.However, the utmost of your time will inescapably be devoted to your child, most probably, If you have a baby while still being in council or at university. also how can you conceivably find enough time for studying?

Taking a gap time or giving up on education is not an option for most Young women currently. At the same time, they find it hard to keep the fine line between studying and being a Mother . Still, there's an indispensable result – you have to learn to ask for help. Be it professional help, like the instructor's backing, or just asking musketeers and family to take off some of the childcare cargo – any option will bring at least some relief!

Mental Health

Giving birth is awful, but it may have some unwelcome consequences concerning a Young mum's internal health. Some women are at an advanced threat of suffering from a number of conditions, including depression, baby blues, and postnatal depression.

Some of the frequently present symptoms are as follow

Mood swings
Trouble eating
Anxiety
Lack of attention
Difficulty sleeping
Inviting fatigue
fear attacks
Difficulty relating with a baby,etc.
Still, the critical thing is to know that you aren't alone and help is always available, If you witness any internal issues caused by parturition. At this point, it's vital to compass yourself with probative people, take good care of your internal good either with the help of specified contemplations or some practices.

Seek out the advice if and when you need it. With the right approach, you'll fluently battle the symptoms!

fiscal Problems

With the birth of a baby, one's life changes a lot, and so do the fiscal requirements. The utmost scholars are living on a tight budget by dereliction. Therefore, when they give birth to a child, lots of fiscal issues may arise. Your requirements will increase doubly as a minimum, and that's a commodity you should be ready for! There are ways for Young parents to save plutocrats. Read my having a baby on a budget for further advice on this.

immaculately, if you can calculate on the fiscal support from family, it can help you avoid the struggle. still, there are a many druthers
. Of course, pupil- mothers will probably not have the possibility to get a full- time position because babies bear nearly 100% of time and

attention. In this situation, a well- paid freelance job can be your stylish bet!

Breastfeeding

Getting a Mother for the first time in your life, you'll hear a lot about the benefits of breastfeeding. Still, one thing that people will probably not tell you is that this process does n't always come naturally as one would anticipate.

There are lots of dilemmas and difficulties related to suckling that you must just accept and try to manage. The stylish thing one can do is examine the issue, take all possible measures to help inconvenient situations, and consult with the specialists if demanded.

Lack of Time

getting Young parents, utmost people start lacking time for literally everything – work, studies, themselves, sleep, and numerous other

effects. still, this is a difficulty faced by all new parents, not just the bones
 who are still at council.

Learn to manage your time wisely! Get on a specific schedule and plan your days in advance to ease the stress and lack of time.

chapter 2 :little or no paid family leave after giving birth or espousing a child

Mother nal leave, or family leave, is a hand benefit available in nearly all countries. The term" Mother nal leave" may include motherliness, Mother nighty, and relinquishment leave; or may be used distinctively from" motherliness leave" and" Maternity leave" to describe separate family leave available to either parent to watch for smallchildren.In some countries and authorities," family leave" also includes leave handed to watch for ill family members. frequently, the minimal benefits and eligibility conditions are questioned by law.

Demonstration for Mother nal leave in the European Parliament

overdue Mother nal or family leave is handed when an employer is needed to hold a hand's job while that hand is taking leave. Paid Mother nal or family leave provides paid time off work to watch for or make arrangements for the welfare of a child or dependent family member. The three most common models of backing are government-mandated social insurance/ social security(where workers, employers, or taxpayers in general contribute to a specific public fund), employer liability(where the employer must pay the hand for the length of leave), and mixed programs that combine both social security and employer liability.

Mother nal leave has been available as a legal right and/ or governmental program for numerous times, in one form or another. In 2014, the International Labour Organization reviewed Mother nal leave programs in 185 countries and homes, and set up that all countries except Papua New Guinea have laws calling some form of Mother n leave.A different study showed that of 186 countries examined, 96 offered some pay to mothers

during leave, but only 44 of those countries offered the same forfathers.The United States, Papua New Guinea, and a many islet countries in the Pacific Ocean are the only countries in the United Nations that don't bear employers to give paid time off for newparents.Private employers occasionally give either or both overdue and paid Mother nal leave outside of or in addition to any legal accreditation.

Research has linked paid Mother nal leave to more health issues for children as well as mothers

goods

generally, the goods of Mother nal leave are advancements in antenatal

and postnatal care, including a drop in child mortality. The goods of Mother nal leave on the labor request include an increase in employment, changes in stipend, and oscillations in the rate of workers returning to work. Leave legislation can also impact fertility rates.

On the labor request

A study in Germany set up that stipend dropped by 18 percent for every time a hand spends on Maternity leave.However, after the original drop in stipend, the hand's payment rebounds faster than the payment of someone not offered Mother nal leave. A study of California's leave policy, the first state in theU.S. to bear employers to offer paid Mother nal leave, showed that stipend did increase.(58)

Mother nal leave can lead to lesser job security.Studies differ in how this helps return to work after taking time off. Some studies show that if a parent is gone for further than a time after the birth of a child, it decreases the possibility that he or she'll return.Other studies of shorter leave ages show that parents no longer need to quit their jobs in order to watch for their children, so employment return increases.

It doesn't appear that Mother nal leave programs have had a significant effect on the gender pay envelope gap, which has remained fairly steady since the late 1980s, despite adding relinquishment of Mother nal leave programs.

Mother and son spend time together
Motherliness leave and its goods

In theU.S., while the Family and Medical Leave Act of 1993(FMLA) allows for overdue Mother nal leave, parents frequently don't use this eligibility to its fullest extent as it's unaffordable. As a result, some studies show that the FMLA has had a limited impact on how important leave new parents take.Though specific quantities can vary, having a child(including the cost of high-quality childcare) costs families roughly$,000 in the first time. These high costs contribute to new mothers

in the United States returning to work hastily than new mothers

in European countries; roughly one third of women in the United States return to work within three months of giving birth, compared to roughly five per cent in theU.K., Germany, and Sweden,(62) and just over half of mothers

in the United States with a child under the age of one work.

There's some substantiation that legislation for Mother nal leave raises the liability of women returning to their former jobs as opposed to changing to a new job. This rise is allowed

to fall to between 10 and 17. contemporaneously, there's a drop in the chance of women who find new jobs, which falls between 6 and 11. Therefore, similar legislation appears to increase how numerous women return to work post-childbirth by around 3 or 4.

Also, it appears that Mother nal leave programs do allow women to stay home longer before returning to work as the probability of returning to an old job falls in the alternate month after parturition before dramatically rising in the third month. Although this legislation therefore appears to have minimal effect on women choosing to take leave, it does appear to increase the time women take in leave.

Motherly leave legislation could pose benefits or detriment to employers. The main implicit debit of commanded leave is its eventuality to disrupt productive conditioning by raising rates of hand absenteeism. With commanded leave for a certain period of time and facing prolonged absence of the mothers
In the plant, enterprises will be faced with two options: hire a temp(which could involve training costs) or function with a missing hand. Alternatively, these programs could be positive for employers who preliminarily didn't offer leave because they were upset about attracting workers who are disproportionately likely to use

maternity leave. Therefore, there's eventuality for these programs to correct request failures.A debit of rising leave at the societal position, still, is the performing drop in the womanish labor force. In countries with a high demand for labor, including numerous present- day countries with growing populations, a lower labor force is inimical.

A commodity important to note for all the exploration cited over is that the results generally depend on how leave content is defined, and whether the programs are for overdue or paid leave. programs guaranteeing paid leave are considered by some to be dramatically more effective than overdue- leave programs.

For women collectively, long breaks in employment, as would come from Mother nal leave, negatively affects their careers. Longer gaps are associated with reduced continuance earnings and lower pension disbursements as well as worsened career prospects and reduced earnings. Due to these downsides, some countries, specially Norway, have expanded family policy enterprise to increase the father's share and expand childcare in an effort to work towards lesser gender equivalency.

Paid family leave provides workers paid and defended time off to watch for an invigorated or family member. Indeed though its physical, internal, and profitable benefits are extensively conceded, theU.S. remains one of only six countries in the world without a public paid family leave program.However, new legislation would give four weeks of paid family leave to all eligible U, If passed and inked intolaw.S. workers, including those who may not else be suitable to go to take time off to watch for their new baby.

What's paid family leave?

Paid family leave is defended, paid time off from work to watch for a family member. Though it's frequently associated with motherliness leave and Maternity leave to be with a invigorated, recently espoused child, or foster child, paid family leave also applies to workers who take time off from work to

Address their own serious health conditions(including gestation)
Care for a family member suffering from a serious health condition
Address family circumstances arising from a military service member's deployment
While civil agencies, nine countries and Washington,D.C., and some private companies offer or will soon begin offering paid family leave benefits, theU.S. is one of only six countries in the world – and the only bucolic nation – that does not have any kind of public paid family leave program in place.(For comparison, new parents in Denmark partake a aggregate of 52 weeks of paid leave after drinking a new child.)

According to theU.S. Bureau of Labor Statistics, only about 23 percent of private workers qualify for some type of private paid family leave through their company. About 60 percent of Americans qualify for 12 weeks of overdue defended time off after the birth, relinquishment or placement of a child through the Family & Medical Leave Act(FMLA). That FMLA leave, along with a combination of short-term disability benefits and holiday

and sick days, is how most new parents in theU.S. cobble together their motherliness and Maternity leaves.

numerous new parents can not go to take important(if any) overdue time at all. One study set up that 23 percent of women in theU.S. return to work within just ten days of having a baby.

Despite not having a paid family leave program, Americans extensively support it – one bean set up that 82 percent of people believe mothers should have paid leave after a birth or relinquishment. Legislation is presently in the workshop that, if passed and inked into law, would introduce four weeks of paid family leave forU.S. workers.

What are the benefits of paid family leave?
The physical, internal, and profitable benefits of maternity leave and Maternity leave are not just anecdotal – they have been showcased in numerous studies for new mothers and non-birthing mates.

Experts have set up numerous benefits to paid family leave, including

Physical benefits of paid family leave

Advanced invigorated vaccination rates.
Lower child mortality rates.
A drop in hospitalizations of mothers
and babies.
An increase in the inauguration and duration of breastfeeding(for nursing mothers).

Mental and emotional benefits of paid family leave

Increased cling with the baby(for both mothers and mates), as well as a lesser engagement in caregiving for the non-birth parent.

A strengthened relationship between both parents.

A lower liability of postpartum depression for new mothers.

profitable benefits of paid family leave

An increased liability that workers, especially mothers, will return to their jobs after leave, performing in lower development for a company.

bettered hand morale.

Reduced fiscal instability and stress for workers.

Access to paid leave would be salutary to people of color, who the data shows, frequently do not indeed have the same access to defended overdue leave as white workers do. Only roughly 39 percent of Black grown-ups and 29 percent of Latino grown-ups are eligible for overdue FMLA leave, compared to 41 percent of white grown-ups.

Women of color are more likely to suffer from poor mother and infant-affiliated health issues – according to the CDC, Black mothers are two to three times more likely than white women to die during gestation or after giving birth. Experts believe paid leave can help constrict these disagreements, furnishing fiscal security and healthcare access to underserved communities.

Who's eligible for paid family leave?

Until paid family leave becomes nationally commanded in theU.S, only a small quantum of Americans are presently eligible for paid family leave, which they admit through state- funded programs or benefits handed by the private companies they work for.

Civil workers admit paid family leave The Federal Employee Paid Leave Act(FEPLA) grants them 12 weeks of paid leave after the birth or placement of a child. There are caveats though FEPLA replaces FMLA for civil workers, so only those eligible for FMLA are entitled to this benefit(meaning those who've been at their job for at least a time). Federal workers must also agree in writing that they'll return to their employer for at least 12 weeks after their leave ends, or threaten having to pay back the costs of their leave.

 workers who live in one of nine countries(plus Washington,D.C.) have or will soon have access to some form of paid family leave, though these programs do not always pay a full payment. State- position paid family leave programs are generally funded through hand- paid payroll levies and administered through a disability insurance program. The countries that presently have paid family leave programs or are planning to soon begin offering them are

California
Colorado
Connecticut
District of Columbia
Massachusetts
New Jersey

New York

Oregon

Rhode Island

Washington

A growing number of private companies offer paid family leave for their workers – about 23 percent of private workers nationally qualify, according to theU.S. Bureau of Labor Statistics. Paid Mother nal leave for these companies varies – for some this means a many months of paid time off after a birth, relinquishment, or surrogacy. For other veritably generous(and rare) pots, the biggest prerequisite is unlimited paid time off for over to one time after drinking a baby.

How is paid family leave different from FMLA?

While both offer job protection(meaning you can not lose your job for taking leave), the main difference between paid family leave and FMLA is that paid family leave is paid, and FMLA isn't.

Not all workers qualify for FMLA leave benefits, either Your company must have further than 50 workers, and if you've had to have worked there for at least a time. But, if a public paid family leave policy is legislated, lawyers anticipate that all workers would be eligible for benefits, anyhow of the size of their employer, how long they have worked there, and whether or not they are a part- or full- time hand. Independent contractors would be eligible under the proposed civil paid leave policy, too.

Also, a public paid family leave policy would most probably broaden the description of family members to include extended family similar to siblings and grandparents. FMLA only gives eligible workers time off to watch for a parent, partner, or child.

Will there ever be paid family leave in theU.S.?
The short answer: Hopefully! Though paid family leave is a major content of current discussion, it's actually been on and off the table in theU.S. for further than a century.

In fact, the conception of paid motherliness leave dates to 1919, when the International Labor Organization's Maternity Protection Convention of 1919 created proffers for motherliness leave. In the decades following the convention, nearly every country except theU.S. officially espoused those proffers, which gave working mothers 12 weeks of paid maternity leave and medical care during and after gestation, plus time off during work to breastfeed, among other benefits.

New legislative framework supported by President Biden's administration would give four weeks of paid leave to private- sector workers, including mothers and non-birthing mates. Known as figure Back More, the legislation firstly called for 12 weeks of paid leave, and its fate is still yet to be determined.However, it could go into effect in 2024, If passed and inked into law.

No matter what happens, advocates for paid leave – and working parents – aren't giving up their fight.

Chapter 3 : moping employer hesitance to offer suckling support or flexible schedules

Support for breastfeeding in the plant includes several types of hand benefits and services, including

writing commercial programs to support breastfeeding women; tutoring workers about breastfeeding; furnishing designated private space for breastfeeding or expressing milk; allowing flexible scheduling to support milk expression during work; giving mothers

options for returning to work, similar as teleworking, part- time work, and extended motherliness leave; furnishing on- point or near- point child care; furnishing high- quality bone pumps; and offering professional lactation operation services and support.

mothers are the swift- growing members of theU.S. labor force.

roughly 70 of employed mothers

with children younger than 3 working full time. One- third of these mothers

return to work within 3 months after birth and two- thirds return within 6 months.Working Outside the home is related to a shorter duration of breastfeeding, and intentions to work full time are significantly associated with lower rates of breastfeeding initiation and shorter duration. Low- income women,

among whom African American and Hispanic women are overrepresented, are more likely than their advanced- income counterparts to return to work before and to be engaged in jobs that make it challenging for them to continue breastfeeding.Given the substantial presence of mothers In the pool, there's a strong need to establish lactation support in the plant.

walls linked in the plant include

a lack of inflexibility for milk

expression in the work schedule, lack of lodgment to pump or store bone- milk, enterprises about support from employers and associates, and

real or perceived low milk force.

mothers who continue suckling after returning to work need the support of their associates, administrators,andothersintheworkplace.Individu al employers can do a great deal to produce an atmosphere that supports workers who breastfeed.Such an atmosphere will come easier to achieve as workplace support programs are promoted to different employers. Plant support programs can be promoted to employers, including directors of mortal coffers, hand health fellow, insurers, and health providers serving numerous of a particular association's workers.

Support programs in the plant have several factors. numerous factors, similar as how numerous women need support and the coffers available, help determine the most applicable factors for a given setting. An outline document developed by the United States Breastfeeding Committee discusses " acceptable, """ expanded, " and " comprehensive " support for breastfeeding in the plant.

essential rudiments of a successful plant program are space, time, support, and doorkeepers. immaculately, a Nursing Mother

Room(NMR) is centrally located with acceptable lighting,
 ventilation, sequestration, seating, a Gomorrah, an electrical outlet, and conceivably a
 refrigerator. Employers can use numerous different strategies to insure time for breastfeeding or milk expression, including flexible work schedules and locales, break times for pumping, and job sharing.

 Factors that impact breastfeeding among working women

 mothers are the swift- growing members of theU.S. pool. In the once 20 times, the chance of new mothers
 in the pool has increased by further than 80 to a current position of 60. One third of working mothers
 return to work within three months of the birth of their child
 and two thirds return within six months. Only 15 of employers offer paid motherliness leave other than short- term disability insurance.

Employment plays a crucial part in a woman's opinions about child feeding. A woman's career plans have the most significant impact on both whether she breastfeeds simply and for how long she breastfeeds.Working outside the home negatively affects both inauguration and duration of breastfeeding.

race

Although motherly employment is a handicap to breastfeeding in all ethnical groups, it's a particular concern in the African- American population. African- American women tend to have lower rates of breastfeeding, return to work sooner, and are more likely to work full- time than other population groups.The need for worksite support is especially pivotal among African- American Mother
Income

underprivileged women with lower income situations appear to have the topmost difficulty combining work and breastfeeding and are frequently employed in low- pay envelope jobs whose settings make continued sucklingdiffcult.The Welfare Reform Act has led to further women returning to work sooner than they had planned, performing in significant issues with maintaining breastfeeding.

Motherliness leave

A 16- country study set up that acceptable motherliness leave programs might increase suckling sufficiently to help one to two neonatal deaths per,000 live births. numerous women in the United States aren't suitable to take a long maternity leave due to fiscal pressures. African American women and women employed in low- pay envelope jobs tend to take shorter maternity leaves.

Although the 1993 Family and Medical Leave Act(FMLA) provides for overdue motherliness leave, numerous women aren't eligible for or don't use this benefit. Only 20 of mothers

in the United States meet the eligibility criteria, which include employment in a plant of further than

workers, working further than 24 hours per week, and employment for at least a time of nonstop service.12 Other women choose not to share in FMLA because they can not go to take overdue leave.

Accommodations in the plant

There's ample substantiation that a probative work point terrain with a private place to express milk and access to a quality bone pump helps women feel more confident in continuing to breastfeed after returning to work, and that lack of lodgment contributes to shorter

suckling duration. Women who don't express milk regularly witness a drop in milk force that leads to early weaning.

Chapter 4 : plant demarcation against new parents, especially mothers

Working mothers
are frequently anticipated to work like they do n't have children and raise children as if they do n't work. This insolvable standard is at the root of gender inequalities in the plant, according to two new Washington University inSt. Louis studies.

The exploration papers, published independently in Demography, demonstrate how

inflexible schedules and prejudiced hiring practices, combined with mothered artistic morals around breadwinning and caregiving, lead to demarcation against mothers
and immortalize gender inequalities in the plant.

" The epidemic further opened our eyes to the struggles that working parents face particularly mothers

" mothers have disproportionately shouldered the burden of caregiving during the epidemic. As a result, they also have been more likely to drop out of the labor force, reduce their work hours or use family leave vittles made possible through the Families First Coronavirus Response Act. And for parents who have been suitable to work ever, their Mother nal status has been more salient than ever ahead with kiddies showing up on drones or being heard in the background.

" My concern is that rather of creating programs to support families, employers will be more likely to distinguish against mothers because they will view them as lower committed to their jobs.

Demarcation in hiring Can mothers
be ideal workers?
former exploration into employer demarcation against mothers
The hiring process has concentrated simply on council- educated women in professional and directorial occupations. Little was known about whether lower educated mothers
navigating the low- pay envelope labor request experience analogous disadvantages.

To study demarcation across the labor request, Dianne conducted a field trial in which she submitted210 fictitious operations to low- pay envelopes and professional/ directorial jobs in sixU.S. metropolises. For each position, she submitted two also good operations. The only difference was that one operation included signals of fatherhood, similar as Parent school teacher Association levy work, while the other operation — also for a womanish seeker —

listed levy work in an association that was unconnected to parenting.

Across occupations, message rates were significantly lower for mothers
than for childless women. In low- pay envelope service jobs,26.7 of the childless women entered a message compared to mothers '21.5. Also,22.6 of the childless womanish aspirants entered calls for professional and directorial positions, compared to 18.4 for mothers.
" The findings demonstrate that demarcation isn't limited to women with council degrees in time- ferocious professional occupations. " Across labor request parts, mothers
appear to be also underprivileged at the hiring stage. "

And the estimates of demarcation against mothers
are likely conservative because childless womanish aspirants don't gesture that they aren't parents. Some employers are likely to assume that these aspirants also have children.

demarcation against mothers

likely results from conflict between the perceived time commitments necessary to be a " good Mother " and an ideal worker. Whereas numerous professional and directorial workers are anticipated to work all the time, low- pay envelope service workers are decreasingly anticipated to work at any time.

" Cultural morals that mothers
will assume primary responsibility for children who are in direct conflict with the morals that workers should be free of family scores. " Employers frequently question mothers
' commitment and capability to work long or variable hours and trips. Not unexpectedly, fathers don't face the same questions. "

Dianne also set up substantiation that employers distinguish further explosively against mothers
when certain demands are listed in job advertisements. In the study, mothers

' probability of entering a message were 5.7,6.6 and 13.6 chance points lower when time pressure, collaboration and trip conditions, independently, were listed in professional/ directorial job advertisements.

" Along with time pressure, collaboration conditions limit inflexibility over when and where work is performed, requiring workers to be around more workers and guests at specific times.

still, they may distinguish further explosively against mothers
when jobs near collaboration, " If employers assume that mothers
will be less suitable to meet inflexible time demands. These types of job demands are especially common in professional and directorial occupations. "

In low- pay envelope service jobs, employers appear to distinguish also against mothers anyhow of whether nonstandard hours similar to nights or weekends are needed. still, when job advertisements indicated scheduling insecurity, mothers

were. chance points less likely to admit a message than childless women.

Are 40- hour work weeks pushing mothers out of the pool?

Dianne studied how the structure and compensation of work hours shapes gender inequality in the labor request. Using individual data from recent, nationally representative panels of the Survey of Income and Program Participation, along with occupational characteristics data from the American Community Survey, Dianne examined the effect of occupational strictness on employment for new mothers , fathers and childless women.

They set up that women who worked in occupations with advanced shares working 40- or- further hours per week and occupations that paid advanced pay envelope decorations for longer hours prior to a first birth were significantly less likely to be employed post-birth. They set up no analogous relationship between inflexible work hours and employment for fathers or childless women.

mothers ' probability of working post-birth depended explosively on their pre-birth occupation. Among women in flexible occupations — defined as those that were 1 standard divagation below average in occupational work hour strictness — an estimated 79.2 of women continued working post-birth. In discrepancy, only67.6 of women in inflexible occupations – those that were 1 standard divagation below average in occupational work hour strictness – continued working post-birth.

"(The) results illustrate how individual employment opinions are concertedly constrained by the structure of the labor request and patient unsexed artistic morals about breadwinning and caregiving.

" strictness in work hours generates work-family conflict that eventually pushes mothers out of the labor force. "

The findings are important because indeed short work interruptions can affect substantial long-term pay envelopes and career costs, and make it delicate for matters to find unborn employment. programs and plant structures that enable further mothers

 to maintain employment post-birth could move the needle on closing the gender- pay envelope gap.

According to Dianne, part- time work isn't a feasible option in utmost careers because company- handed health insurance is contingent upon working full time and hourly rates are frequently cut mainly for part- time workers.

In discrepancy, numerous European countries have reduced their standard full- time workweek to a more family-friendly range below 40 hours. Also, workers in these countries have the right to reduce work hours without fear of losing their job or facing demarcation. Not concurrently, women's employment is advanced in countries with programs that support flexible work time.

" Our exploration shows that unsexed patterns of work in the home and labor request continue to be shaped by artistic morals that tie motherhood primarily to full- time employment and fatherhood to time- ferocious, child-centered caregiving.

Despite a large proportion of working mothers in the American pool, exploration suggests that negative conceptions and demarcation against working mothers
continue to live. In a set of two experimental studies, the current paper examined subtle demarcation against non-pregnant, working mothers
in different hiring settings. In Study 1, using a between- subject field trial and applying for geographically dispersed jobs with manipulated resumes, we set up substantiation for subtle

demarcation, similar that mothers entered more negativity in message dispatches than women without children, men without children, and fathers. They were also rejected more snappily than women without children and fathers. In Study 2, using a more controlled experimental paradigm, we tested our thesis in an academic interview evaluation setting. We set up that mothers

faced more interpersonal hostility across different job types as compared to women without children. Together, these studies punctuate the presence of subtle demarcation against working mothers

at different stages of the hiring process.

Throwing further light on Demarcation Against Working mothers in the Hiring Process exploration indicates that mothers

witness advanced situations of demarcation across different employment settings, both formally(e.g., in pay, hiring, and creation openings) and interpersonally(e.g., inconsideration, hostility), as compared to fathers, men without children, and women without children. The obstacles that mothers faces at work are frequently pertained to as the " motherly wall, " which is a tropical manacle to working women's success once they've children. As roughly 80 – 90 of women will come mothers during their continuance and a maturity(70) of mothers who have children under 18 are employed, there are wide social and profitable counter accusations to the plant demarcation that mothers face. Given this pervasive miracle, a growing body of exploration has examined mechanisms through which demarcation against mothers occurs. Social part proposition posits that women are prescribed rates associated with the caregiving part. harmonious with this notion, due to their caregiving places, mothers are frequently perceived to be less competent, warmer, and less married to work than women without children In turn, these negative conceptions may manifest as negative treatment toward mothers in both subtle and overt forms. Although motherhood status doesn't appear to negatively affect working men, mothers

are less likely to be hired, called back for an interview, given training openings, and more likely to be recommended for lower hires as compared to non-mothers

Despite these findings, extant exploration has substantially concentrated on further overt forms of demarcation against working mothers , neglecting the more nebulous but inversely mischievous form of demarcation that mothers may witness. Due to evolving social stations and changing civil rights laws, this further contemporary form of demarcation frequently manifests in lower intensity, subtle actions that are more delicate to describe and can be masked as accidental. The many studies that have examined subtle demarcation against working mothers

concentrate on the guests of pregnant women. The conceptions of pregnant women partake in some parallels with post-birth mothers , but there are also some differences between the two.

gestation is a dynamic smirch that changes visibility and stability over time, while fatherhood is a endless yet potentially concealable smirch

As similar, the current paper aims to examine subtle demarcation against non-pregnant working mothers using a set of two experimental studies that examine the gists of working mothers across different stages of the hiring process capsule screening and interview evaluation. In the first study, exercising a between- subject field experimental design, we proposed and tested whether subtle demarcation against working mothers exists in the form of communication negativity and reject speed during the capsule screening stage. In the alternate study, extending findings from the field trial that uncovered substantiation of subtle demarcation against working mothers , we examined the extent to which the same demarcation manifests against working mothers when being estimated for job felicity in interview evaluation settings.

This book makes two important benefits to organizational education. First, by fastening on subtle demarcation against working mothers , we examine an important but frequently understudied part of mothers '(rather than pregnant women's) guests in hiring settings. Work on plant demarcation against post-birth mothers has largely concentrated on overt and formal demarcation similar to hiring and performance evaluation issues which only provides a partial picture of these workers ' guests . Given that subtle demarcation can be as poignant as overt demarcation, especially when being chronically it's essential to examine the full diapason of mothers ' plant guests .

Alternatively, we borrow a robust methodological approach by examining our exploration question experimentally in both laboratory and non-laboratory settings. In Study 1, we use a field trial design with experimentally manipulated resumes to apply for geographically dispersed jobs in colorful diligence. In doing so, we advance the methodology used in former hiring demarcation studies, which are substantially conducted in laboratories or the field within a particular assiduity and geographical region. In Study 2, our use of a more controlled experimental paradigm extends our Study 1 findings to the interview evaluation setting and allows for examining possible boundary conditions. Our coupling of these reciprocal approaches increases internal and external validity and maximizes the robustness and generalizability of our findings. Together, this brace of studies exfoliate light on the frequently- overlooked instantiations of demarcation against non-pregnant working mothers

Defining Subtle and Overt Demarcation
Popular exchanges about demarcation primarily concentrate on its further obvious forms, similar as being passed over for a desirable job assignment, not being hired, or indeed passing violence related to a stigmatized social identity. All of these examples reflect overt demarcation, or " explicitly negative address and/ or treatment

legislated toward social nonages on the base of their nonage status class ". Examples of overt demarcation include bullying, hostile sexism, and hostile racism. Overt demarcation is clear in intention and can be done formally or interpersonally. Targets and spectators can fluently fete overt demarcation as a response to a certain stigmatized social identity. Accordingly, due to evolving societal stations and adding civil rights protections over the once many decades, numerous forms of overt demarcation are now illegal and generally supposed inferior by the public. Commonly, overt demarcation is related to negative consequences, such as lower favorable career issues, poorer physical and internal health, and advanced development.

In discrepancy, subtle demarcation can be defined as negative actions nebulous in intent and can be legislated purposely or unconsciously due to targets ' nonage status class. Examples of subtle demarcation include everyday racism, benevolent sexism, and inconsideration. Subtle demarcation can be done formally or interpersonally, and its defining characteristic is being vague in intention and thus fluently masked as trivial or inoffensive. For example, inconsideration, similar to being intruded mid-conversation, endured by targets can be brushed off as general rudeness or lack of courtesy. Because of its nebulous nature, subtle demarcation is frequently delicate to identify and is thus not unlawful or extensively socially condemned. Nonetheless, exploration has suggested that subtle demarcation is at least inversely, if not further, mischievous to targets ' work and health issues and may also do more chronically. When coupled with its nebulous nature, it can place targets in a harmonious state of discomfort, which can deplete their coffers and influence crucial work and particular issues. Next, we will bandy the theoretical background of demarcation against working mothers

and empirical attestations for its subtle instantiations.

Hiring Demarcation Against Working mothers

Theoretical explanations for plant demarcation against mothers

can be predicated in status characteristics proposition and social part proposition. Status characteristics proposition contends that when one social order is more socially valued than another the social order becomes a status characteristic and members of the valued group are regarded as having lesser worth and capability. Following this line of sense, the fatherhood penalty thesis proposes that fatherhood, due to mothers' part as primary caregivers, is a socially devalued status in the environment of work. Given this socially devalued status at work, mothers

are viewed as lower good and competent, and thus less desirable as job campaigners.

Likewise, the social part proposition contends that gender- grounded conceptions are deduced from the traditional distribution of labor between men and women. Specifically, men are generally specified breadwinner places, while women are specified caregiving places. As a result, people are anticipated to retain characteristics that will enable them to succeed in their separate prescribed places; men are anticipated to be assertive, independent, and competitive, while women are anticipated to be nurturing, warm, and relationship- acquainted. Extending social part proposition, part congruence proposition asserts that women are treated more negatively in the plant because their professional places are incongruent with their specified caregiving places. Because the professional part is characterized by manish characteristics similar to fierceness and independence(i.e., characteristics that men are anticipated to formerly have), women are viewed as lacking the necessary skills to succeed as professionals. Taken together, these propositions suggest that being a Mother is a devalued social characteristic in the work environment that signals incapacity. Mothers who work outside of the home defy traditional gender prospects, which results in negative, prejudiced responses. thus, people frequently anticipate working mothers to be less suitable for their professional places and treat Mothers more negatively in the work environment.

It's also important to note that although the theoretical base of demarcation against postpartum working mothers
and pregnant workers are analogous, the guests of these two groups of women aren't identical. gestation is a dynamic smirch, and its adding visibility can increase the salience of women's feminity. Likewise, gestation can be viewed as disruptive and unstable depending on a Mother's health throughout her gestation. In discrepancy,post-birth fatherhood tends to be viewed as a more stable and endless smirch that's also unnoticeable because of its lack of physical incarnation. As instanced by literature in other social wisdom fields(e.g., sociology, economics), demarcation against Mothers
isn't limited to pregnant women as experimenters have set up difference in work issues between post-birth mothers

and other social groups thus, we argue that fatherhood status is qualitatively different from gestation status and graces separate attention.

Empirical substantiation has largely supported these reciprocal theoretical fabrics by changing that Mothers face pervasive negative conceptions and demarcation in professional settings. Because meters are presumed to carry the primary caregiver part, they're perceived as less available and agentic thannon-caregiving parents, which are generally men. Compared to fathers and women without children, mothers are viewed as lower married and less competent but warmer. These negative conceptions can manifest in overt demarcation toward mothers in colorful work settings, similar as hiring, pay, and creation. For illustration, one of the first studies on hiring demarcation against mothers was an inspection study of account enterprises, where manipulated resumes that only differed by gender and Mother nal status were transferred out to apply for counting positions. Results showed that women were less likely to be called back than men, and mothers were less likely to be called back than women without children. An alternate, more recent study used the same methodology of applying to job openings announced in an original review and set up the same pattern of results. Mothers were less likely to admit calls than non-mothers. farther experimental substantiation set up that mothers

were estimated as lower competent, married, and immediate, and as a result, less likely to be recommended for hire.

Indeed though there's a substantial body of substantiation that mothers

witness hiring demarcation, recent exploration suggests that similar overt instantiations of demarcation may not be as rampant as they were in former decades. For example, recent field experimental substantiation indicated that pregnant job aspirants didn't witness differences in message rates in retail or professional jobs. One possible explanation is that overt forms of demarcation grounded on coitus and Mother nal status are frequently illegal. Still, negative comprehensions of working mothers haven't faded, and they may manifest in more subtle, nebulous mores. Indeed, there's little oversight or formal laws and regulations proscribing subtle demarcation compared to overt demarcation. While people may try to avoid overt demarcation in employment settings, exploration has shown that attempts to suppress negative conceptions can affect demarcation arising in the form of subtly negative actions. therefore, if observers inhibit themselves from engaging in overt demarcation, their negativity toward working mothers

may rather surface in the form of subtle demarcation.

In support of this theoretical logic, substantiation from field trials has shown that the same woman applying for retail jobs endured more rudeness and hostility when she was wearing a gestation prosthesis than when she wasn't visibly pregnant. Similar subtle demarcation isn't limited to retail settings; analogous results were also observed when pregnant women applied for professional jobs,

which aren't as low paying or physically demanding as retail jobs. Although our focus is on post-birth mothers , conceptions of pregnant women are analogous to those of mothers , and pregnant women are anticipated to fulfill traditional places associated with mothers . thus, it's reasonable to anticipate similar negative treatment to extend beyond giving birth when mothers
remain in the pool.

Indeed, beyond the hiring environment, exploration has set up that mothers
are perceived as lower likable, less desirable as associates, and more interpersonally hostile. In addition, directors perceive mothers as having an advanced position of work- family conflict, indeed when controlling for factual hand experience of work- family conflict. Likewise, mothers witness adding quantities of hostility and inconsideration(e.g., entering insulting reflections) in the plant as the number of children they've increases. Given this body of substantiation, it's logical to infer that mothers may witness subtle demarcation in the hiring

environment. Despite this substantiation, extant exploration on non-pregnant mothers largely focuses on overt, formal issues, similar as payment, hiring recommendation, and allotment of training openings. Thus, erecting on once work on demarcation against pregnant aspirants, we posit that mothers are likely to witness subtle demarcation in on-face-to-face hiring settings, similar as through message dispatches and evaluations. We argue that subtle demarcation in these settings, although not entered by mothers

in real- time, can still have negative goods. For case, because message dispatches are fairly standardized and neutrally articulated, negative dispatches may stand out further prominently. Also, being rejected more snappily may gesture to mothers that they aren't considered as serious aspirants. Eventually, hiring directors may display interpersonal hostility not only in the interview evaluation process, but also in posterior concessions when they make the job offers. Considering the job hunt process involves applying for numerous jobs, the accretive effect of these subtle pointers of demarcation can be mischievous to mothers . Altogether, we propose that

thesis
Working mothers
will witness a advanced degree of subtle demarcation in the hiring environment than women without children, fathers, and men without children.

Study 1 system

Experimental Manipulations
We employed a 2(gender joker or womanish) × 2(Mother nal status parent or non-parent) between- subjects design.Two real resumes with original qualifications(Master's degree, eight times of experience in an critic position, and original leadership experience, awards, chops, and capacities) were used for the manly and womanish operations. The womanish and manly names used on the operations were common Caucasian names. Following former work in this area the aspirant's Mother nal status was

manipulated by indicating their class as a " member of the Northern Virginia Parents Association "(among a list of other conditioning) and briefly mentioning them as having a family in the summary section of the capsule(" I'm willing to dislocate with my family "). In thenon-parent condition, the aspirant was described as an original neighborhood association member and didn't mention family in the summary section(" I'm willing to dislocate "). In total, we transferred out 1008 operations(252 operations per condition for four conditions). Still, because some of the positions were later canceled, we removed 115 operations from our data, performing 893 operations in the final analysis.

Pre-Testing the Resumes

The resumes were pre-tested using a sample of 179 working grown-ups with hiring experience. Actors were aimlessly shown one of the resumes and also asked to estimate the capsule on a series of particulars, including capability, inflexibility, commitment, hireability, warmth, and likability.

Results showed that the manly and womanish performances of the resumes were viewed as original, and the Mother nal status manipulations were successful. Full results and details of the pre-testing procedure are handed in AppendixA.

Design and Procedure

We submitted job operations to online job openings and varied information on the aspirants ' resumes regarding gender and Mother nal status. Subtle demarcation was measured by time ceased from operation to response, the length of the correspondence, and independent coders ' conditions of the positivity and negativity of the response.

Major career hunt websites, similar asIndeed.com,Monster.com, andCareerBuilder.com, were used to detect job openings that matched the qualifications of the aspirants portrayed in our pre-tested resumes.Indeed.com was the most constantly used website(76.56) because it contains the most comprehensive list of job openings attained by continually searching thousands of other websites to collect new bulletins. Resumes were submitted to jobs that fit the qualifications of the aspirant(eight times of experience, Master's degree, business/ exploration/ data critic background). The hunt terms included " business critic/ associate, " " data critic/ associate, " " exploration critic/ associate, " and " adviser " fresh conditions included were that the jobs must be located within the USA, bear at least a bachelorette's degree, and the opening must be posted by the hiring company(as opposed to a contracted hiring agency). Because the academic aspirant address is located in the Washington,D.C. area, we applied to positions each over the country except theD.C. metropolitan area. This assured all jobs applied to needed relocation, thus barring that as an alternate explanation. Two experimenters had to agree that each job was a good fit before an operation was submitted. Each job operation was aimlessly assigned one of the four possible resumes(i.e., between- subject conditions) to rule out any selection effect regarding the assiduity, geographic areas, occupation, or company size that may dispose of our results. In addition, all job descriptions were saved. Two independent coders rated each job description on a variety of criteria, including educational conditions, the number of times of experience needed, and match for aspirant's chops, education, and experience. The coders ' conditions were harmonious. Therefore, a scale was formed by comprising the two conditions and also across the three confines(experience, education, and chops) for a compound measure of qualification match. We also collected the following information about each posting geographic position of the position, assiduity, company size, and gender diversity of the board. These associations are dispersed throughout the country(27.5 Northeast,24.13 South,21.9 Midwest,20.1 West Coast) from a variety of diligence. Over 60 of those associations are intimately possessed or accessories. Over 60 of the associations have a board of directors, with a mean chance of womanish board members of 20.84. Size of the associations ranged from 10 to 2.2 million workers. As can be seen in our correlation matrix, the chance of womanish board members and the number of workers in the association aren't significantly identified to any of our dependent variables of interest except for response time for calls.

Independent Variables
The independent variables were gender(manly or womanish) and Mother nal status(non-parent or parent).

Dependent Variables
Subtle demarcation was measured by 1) rejection speed(i.e., the time ceased between operation and rejection in days), 2) length of response dispatches in characters(via dispatch or phone), and 3) positivity and negativity of the response communication. Because message dispatches can be conceptualized as a form of commerce from the hiring associations and are similar to hiring directors ' in- person actions in an interview environment, we determine that analogous positivity and negativity measures are applicable to assess the quality of the message

dispatches. We reason callback communication quality(in both length and choice of words tone reflected) is a suggestion of subtle demarcation because message dispatches are generally fairly neutral for professional purposes. Thus, negative dispatches may stand out prominently to aspirants as an nebulous, low intensity form of negative treatment. Also, rejection speed can be perceived as the degree to which aspirants are seriously considered for the condition. Thus, we suppose them to be applicable measures for subtle demarcation in the capsule screening environment.

Two independent coders eyeless to the conditions(after junking of all language that indicates the gender of the aspirant from message dispatches) enciphered all of the responses for negativity(enthusiastic, friendly, warm, polite, comfortable, interested, negative, hostile, irked, nervous) on a scale from 1 to 5(1 = not at all; 5 = a great deal), and the positive adjective particulars were latterly reverse-enciphered. These particulars were acclimated from former field studies measuring interpersonal treatment. There was thickness across coders, and thus the parts of those conditions were employed for the analysis.

Study 1 Results

We entered 71 positive and 196 negative calls, which resulted in a total message rate of 29.80(and a positive message rate of 7.92). Based on our coding of job descriptions to match aspirants ' experience, education, and chops, the mean compound score for match of job qualifications was 3.89 out of 5, indicating a good fit of qualification between the capsule and the job advertisement. We conducted a 2(gender joker or womanish) × 2(Mother nal status on-parent or parent) ANOVA on the job descriptions ' compound conditions. Results showed that the aspirants ' qualifications were a good fit for the jobs they applied for. Also, the position of the qualification match didn't vary across conditions or relate with any of our dependent variables of interest.

Our thesis prognosticate that mothers

witness more subtle demarcation than women without children, fathers, and men withoutchildren.We conducted a two- way factorial ANOVA(with gender and Mother nal status as IVs) to compare rejection speed, response length, and negativity of the dispatches between those entered by mothers

and those entered by women without children, fathers, and men without children. Results showed that gender and Mother nal status didn't interact to prognosticate negativity of responses.

In light of this non-significant finding, we conducted a post-hoc analysis to examine the factor structure of the construct negativity of response. Results indicated that the two- factor structure was a statistically better fit than the one- factor structure, suggesting that it may be more applicable to divide the negativity measure into two confines positivity andnegativity.ICCs for both positivity and negativity measures indicated sufficient thickness across coders, so the parts of those conditions were employed for the analysis. Results showed that gender and Mother nal status didn't interact to prognosticate positivity of responses. still, gender and Mother nal status interacted to prognosticate negativity of responses, as measured by the new, more terse measure of negativity, similar that mothers

entered more negativity in their calls than women without children, fathers, and men without children. We further conducted a series of independent sample t- tests to compare mothers

to each of the other groups(i.e.,non-mothers, fathers, andnon-fathers) in response to negativity. Results showed that mothers

witness significantly further negativity than non-mothers,on-fathers, andnon-fathers.

Negativity in message dispatches by gender and Mother nal status

There was no significant commerce between gender and Mother nal status on length of responses. Still, gender and Mother nal status also interacted to prognosticate rejection speed.

mothers were rejected more snappily than women without children and fathers. still, they aren't rejected significantly more snappily than men with children. We further conducted a series of independent sample t- tests to compare mothers to each of the other groups(i.e.,non-mothers, fathers, andnon-fathers) in rejection speed. mothers are rejected more snappily than non-mothers, fathers, though not significantly different from non-fathers. Therefore, our thesis was incompletely supported.

Rejection speed by gender and Mother nal status

Study 1 Discussion

The purpose of Study 1 was to determine whether subtle demarcation against working mothers

crop during the capsule screening process. Our results handed some substantiation of subtle demarcation against mothers

during the operation process, similar that mothers

were treated with further negativity in response dispatches and also rejected more snappily than fathers and women without children. Though not differing in rejection speed, mothers

still entered more negative dispatches thannon-fathers do. Altogether, despite the fairly scripted nature of message communication, working mothers

still incurred more subtle discriminative treatment than other aspirants.

suddenly, we didn't find any significant difference among men and women with and without children in communication negativity. This may be due to a dimension issue of the negativity measure, as it contains both negative adjectives and reverse- enciphered positive adjectives. Although this is harmonious with former exploration using this measure, we argued that it may not be applicable to combine both appreciatively and negatively articulated particulars in one measure, as the absence of positivity doesn't always indicate the presence of negativity and vice versa. Indeed, our factor analysis of the negativity measures supports this, similar that the data showed a better model fit with a two- factor structure than a single factor. Thus, we separated the negativity measure into two confines and anatomized them independently.

Our results revealed no difference in message communication positivity, though mothers
do admit further negativity in dispatches than men and women without children. One possible explanation is that message dispatches tend to be fairly neutral to maintain professionalism. The subtle differences in negativity between mothers
and other groups are likely driven by implicit bias against mothers
(e.g., being less married, less competent), similar that the negativity is expressed without the person being conscious of that. Otherwise, in utmost scripts that don't involve working Mother aspirants, hiring directors may just maintain a neutral tone(i.e., neither positive nor negative) because that's standard in professional communication, and those without negative

conceptions that are associated with fatherhood are treated as regular aspirants.

Study 2

There were several limitations from Study 1 that we essay to address in Study 2. First, Study 1 was concentrated on one particular profession at the capsule screening stage, limiting the generalizability to other job diligence and stages of hiring. Second, it's possible that our manipulation of Mother nal status, though effective, might be demonstrated as individualities being involved in caretaking places by getting involved in parent- related conditioning rather than simply indicating Mother nal status. Eventually, adding reliance on technology similar to artificial intelligence during capsule webbing may affect the results of our study.

As a result, we sought to extend our findings from Study 1 by examining the guests of subtle demarcation during interview evaluation in an experimental study. Specifically, we examined the degree to which subtle demarcation occurs against working mothers at the coming stage of the hiring process after capsule screening interview evaluation. Being substantiation for subtle demarcation endured by mothers

is substantially concentrated on gestation. Still, as mentioned before, gestation and post-birth fatherhood are qualitatively different tests for women. The first is dynamic in visibility and disruptiveness but temporary, while the ultimate is unnoticeable but endless. likewise, the current understanding of demarcation faced by post-birth working mothers

is substantially on overt, formal issues, similar as payment recommendations and allotment of interview openings. As mentioned before, given the evolving social and legal geography related to civil rights, it's reasonable to anticipate bias against fatherhood will manifest in subtle ways as well. Thus, we extend our findings from Study 1, which focuses on written communication from associations during the capsule screening stage, by fastening on evaluations in the coming step of the hiring process interviews. Specifically, we anticipate that during interview evaluations(when people are given further unshaped information about the aspirants), mothers

 will continue to be viewed negatively because they witness the same conceptions as pregnant mothers

, similar as being viewed as lower competent, married, and flexible, which can affect subtle demarcation.

likewise, we aim to address the limitations of our Study 1 by examining two possible boundary conditions for demarcation against working mothers

job gender type and modality. Grounded on part congruity propositions, women, especially mothers, may be seen as lower fit for jobs that are more traditionally mannish(e.g., auto deals, account, engineering) as opposed to womanlike(e.g., apparel deals, mortal coffers, gender studies) because their feminity is perceived to be deranged with the virility necessary to succeed in those jobs. thus, we reason that mothers face more subtle demarcation during the hiring process for further mannish jobs as opposed to womanlike bones . Also, women traditionally shoulder a disproportionate quantum of caregiving liabilities, and society also perceives them to be the main caregiver for their children(Eagly, 1987). This was aggravated during the recent COVID- 19 epidemic when mothers had to assume utmost homeschooling and childcare liabilities, as large portions of the pool came remote and children had to attend academy nearly from home. As a family-friendly accommodation once swung to a nonage of workers and maybe stigmatized, remote work has come the norm. Having at least one parent working from home has become a necessity for numerous families because all other forms of childcare support are unapproachable. As mothers

are anticipated to be primarily responsible for childcare, we posit that mothers

who indicate they're available for in- person work may be subject to more subtle demarcation during the hiring process since they're seen as violating their specified caregiving part.

Study 2 styles

party

We signed 950 working grown-ups through Amazon's Mechanical Turk to share in this trial. To identify applicable actors and describe inattention, we included pre screening qualification questions and an attention check question in the check. Actors were needed to be 18 times of age or aged, employed for at least 20 h per week, and abiding in the USA. The final analysis included 888 actors(53 women) after removing responses that failed attention or manipulation checks. The average age of the actors was 37 times old, and about half of the actors indicated they were a parent(50.8). The maturity of actors were Caucasian(75.1), with an 8.9 African American,7.6 Asian,5.7 Hispanic, and2.7 Other. Actors entered$1.50 for completing the check.

Experimental Design and Procedure

The current study glasses the protocol used in Hebl et al. and used a 2(gender of aspirant joker or womanish) × 2(Mother nal status of aspirant parent or non-parent) × 2(job gender type mannish or womanlike) × 2(job modality remote-only or available in- person) between-subjects design. First, actors were asked to imagine themselves as employment placement agents and read a brief description of an aspirant's interview. Specifically, actors read, " We're interested in understanding job placement processes. Please imagine that you work for an employment placement agency and read the following aspirant profile. You'll be asked to recall this profile and give your evaluations concerning job felicity and job placement." also, depending on the condition to which the party was aimlessly assigned, they were handed with an interview summary that described the aspirant as a " woman/ man seeking full- time employment in a position suiting her/ his capacities(who) didn't express interest in any one particular type of job but did express enthusiasm to apply her/ his active work ethic anywhere and can learn snappily. During the interview process, the aspirant was immediate,

gracious, andarticulate.However, the aspirant stated that she could start incontinently, If hired. The aspirant came across as veritably responsible and friendly during the interview. ” Half of the actors were aimlessly assigned to the parent condition, and their interview summary included, “ When asked how she he spends her/ his spare time, the aspirant replied that she he enjoys spending time with his woman
/ her hubby and children. ” The remaining half of the actors were aimlessly assigned to thenon-parent condition, and their interview summary included, “ When asked how she he spends her/ his spare time, the aspirant replied that he she and her hubby/ his woman
 enjoy decorating their new house. ” The actors were also aimlessly assigned to the modality condition and told, “ This aspirant is only available for remote/ in- person work. ”

Actors were also instructed to assess the aspirant for six jobs, assuming that the academic aspirant has the necessary credentials and qualifications for the position. Half of the actors were aimlessly assigned to the " womanlike " condition. They estimated the aspirant for a variety of positions, including those of a family counsel, kindergarten school teacher, apparel store client service associate, pediatrician, women and gender studies professor, and mortal coffers associate. The other half of the actors were aimlessly assigned to the " mannish " condition. These actors estimated aspirants on an array of resemblant positions similar as a commercial counsel, high academy calculation schoolteacher, auto dealership client service associate, psychiatrist, structural engineering professor, and counting associate. Actors were also asked to indicate the extent to which they agreed with particulars that measured perceived job felicity and interpersonal hostility toward the aspirant.

Manipulation Check

Actors were asked about the aspirant's family situation(" Please indicate the aspirant's family situation: woman without children, woman with children, man without children, or man with children ") and whether the aspirant was available for in- person work. 62 responses were removed from the main thesis testing due to incorrect answers to the manipulation check questions.

Measures

Independent Variables

The independent variables are the gender of the aspirant(manly or womanish), the Mother nal status of the aspirant(parent or non-parent), job gender type(mannish or womanlike), and job modality(in- person or remote only).

Dependent Variables

Subtle Demarcation was operationalized as interpersonal hostility and job felicity conditions. Because the setting of this study didn't involve any direct communication between the perceiver and academic aspirant, using the same positivity and negativity measures employed in Study 1 as pointers of subtle demarcation would be unhappy. For case, it may not be as meaningful to measure perceivers ' ' unease " toward the academic seeker described in an interview profile. Thus, we rather espoused the measure of subtle demarcation employed by the experimental paradigm on which the study was grounded. Specifically, we used the seven- item interpersonal hostility measure from Hebl et al. to capture actors ' interpersonal hostility toward the fictitious aspirants. The actors used a 7- point scale(1 = explosively differ; 7 = explosively agree) to indicate their position of agreement with each item. Specifically, actors responded to particulars that described the aspirant as(a) " a lazy worker, "(b) " would complain a lot, "(c) " would try to get out of doing work, "(d) " would anticipate to have their work done for them, " and(e) " would be too temperamental to be an effective worker, " and that the party(f) " would be angry if I had to work with this aspirant, " and(g) " would n't give this person a position of power. " Job felicity was rated on a single item for each of the six positions' ' Do you suppose the aspirant is suitable for the following positions? " on a scale from 1 to 5(1 = surely not; 5 = surely yes). We reason that indeed though these pointers of subtle demarcation won't be directly perceived by aspirants at the interview evaluation stage, it still reflects bias and may indeed manifest again during the concession process after offers are being made, when it would directly impact mothers

Study 2 Results

Descriptive statistics for the crucial variables of interest can be set up in Table 3. For our thesis testing, we conducted a 2(gender of aspirant joker or womanish) × 2(Mother nal status of aspirant parent or non-parent) × 2(job gender type mannish or womanlike) × 2(job modality in- person or remote) between- subject ANCOVA on each of the dependent variables of interests job felicity and interpersonal hostility. All analyses include gender and Mother nal status of the party as control variables.

Results indicated there was a significant commerce between gender and Mother nal status of the aspirant on interpersonal hostility, similar that mothers endured more interpersonal hostility than non-mothers, while on-fathers endured more interpersonal hostility than fathers did. Post hoc independent samples t- test indicated that mothers are estimated with advanced interpersonal hostility compared to non-mothers and fathers, though not significantly different from non-fathers. relations among gender of aspirant, Mother nal status, and job gender type or job modality weren't significant. Also, there were no significant relations among our crucial variables of interest on job felicity. The only exception was gender of the aspirant and job gender type interacting to impact liability to hire, similar that women were more likely to be offered a womanlike type than mannish compartmented professions. Therefore, our thesis was incompletely supported.

Study 2 Interpersonal hostility by aspirant gender and Mother nal status
Study 2 Discussion
We conducted Study 2 for two primary reasons. First, we wanted to determine whether the

patterns of subtle demarcation observed in Study 1 at the capsule screening stage with job aspirants also occur in the interview evaluation process. Second, we examined two fresh boundary conditions that may impact hiring demarcation against working mothers

 job gender type and job modality. harmonious with our findings from Study 1, our analyses suggest that mothers

 suffer subtle demarcation during interview evaluation, similar to actors indicating advanced rates of interpersonal hostility when assessing mothers. Also, this pattern of results held indeed when counting for job gender type and job modality, which further bolsters the robustness of our finding. We further set up support for women being more likely to be offered a woman like- compartmented profession than a mannish bone This corroborated with once exploration that suggests women are seen as not having the necessary rates to succeed in a professional part, especially when the job type is more stereotypically mannish.

Theoretical and Practical Counter Accusations

Altogether, this book contributes to a growing body of exploration that suggests ultramodern demarcation frequently manifests in more subtle ways because it's illegal to exorbitantly distinguish in formal settings and socially inferior to distinguish grounded on non-job-related characteristics. By expressing bias through lower perceptible ways, people can still be perceived as conforming to morals and not violating the prospects for egalitarianism. Indeed, people may have tried to suppress their negative stations and conceptions against mothers that eventually still crop in subtler forms in lower structured settings. Our findings extend former affiliated exploration that focuses on subtle demarcation against mothers across different employment settings. The fact that there's some substantiation of subtle demarcation, despite the largely structured environment of hiring evaluations, is a important index of the continuity of demarcation against working mothers These less egregious penalties for fatherhood status may extend beyond hiring

as women enter the associations, as suggested by previous literature that set up mothers
 facing mistreatment at work.

Chapter 5 : finding affordable, quality child care(especially for babe)

 Child care, else known as day care, is the care and supervision of a child or multiple children at a time, whose periods range from two weeks of age to eighteen times. Child care is a broad content that covers a wide diapason of professionals, institutions, surroundings, conditioning, and social and artistic conventions. Beforehand child care is an inversely important and frequently overlooked element of a child's development.

 A daycare in America

Care eased by analogous-aged children covers a variety of experimental and cerebral goods in both caregivers and charge. This is due to their internal development being in a particular case of not being suitable to progress as it should be at their age.This caregiving part may also be taken on by the child's extended family. Another form of childcare that's on the rise in discrepancy to domestic care paying is that of center- grounded child care. In lieu of domestic care giving, these liabilities may be given to paid caretakers, orphanages or foster homes to give care, casing, and training.

Professional caregivers work within the environment of a center- grounded care(including crèches, daycare, preschools and seminaries) or a home- grounded care(babysitters or family daycare). The maturity of child care institutions available bear child care providers to have extensive training in first aid and be CPR certified. In addition, background checks, medicine testing at all centers, and reference verifications are typically a demand. Child care can correspond to advanced literacy surroundings that include early nonage education or abecedarian education." The ideal of the program of diurnal conditioning should be to foster incremental experimental progress in a healthy and safe terrain and should be flexible to capture the interests of the children and the individual capacities of the children. In numerous cases the applicable child care provider is a schoolteacher or person with educational background in child development, which requires a more focused training away from the common core chops typical of a child caregiver.

As well as these licensed options, parents may also choose to find their own caregiver or arrange child care exchanges barters with another family.
While no bone
 can replace you, quality child care will offer your child a stimulating, nurturing terrain which should help prepare him for academy and to reach his full eventuality.

So what exactly is quality child care? Well, quality is defined as a degree of excellence. This means not average, not " it will do " child care, but excellent child care. nethermost line, you need to feel that the child care provider you elect will offer a safe and stimulating, loving terrain in which your child will mentally and physically thrive.

Characteristics of quality
As you begin your hunt, then what to look for in quality child care

Settings that are safe and give small group sizes and adult- to- child rates encouraging the stylish openings for development; Caregivers or preceptors who have experience and are trained in early nonage development; Settings that offer openings for meaningful parent involvement;
literacy accouterments and tutoring styles that are age-applicable and regardful of children's artistic and ethnical heritage; and Learning openings that promote your child's success in academia.

Child care is a broad term used to describe any number of arrangements or settings where the primary responsibility is minding for Young children. There are as numerous different settings as there are delineations of quality in child care. The number of Young children under the age of five who are watched for during part of the day by grown-ups other than their custodial parents has increased dramatically since 1980, due in large part to an increase in mothers
joining the pool.

According to the 2002 Quality Counts check conducted by Education Week, roughly six out of every ten children, or nearly 12 million children, age five and youngish, are being concertedly watched for by parents and early nonage preceptors, cousins, or other child- care providers.

While numerous parents may prefer to stay home with their babies or Young children, this isn't a fiscal option for the utmost. The United States, unlike numerous other nations, doesn't have a paid Mother nal leave plan for workers after the birth of a baby. This forces numerous families to return to work incontinently and necessitates the need for importing child- care options. Parents are forced to make child- care choices grounded on family fiscal coffers, the vacancy or position of child care, hours of operation, or other factors not inescapably associated with quality. It isn't uncommon to hear of a Mother calling child- care centers to get on waiting lists before calling family members to partake in the joyous news that she's awaiting. Waiting lists for quality programs can be times long, and some families may Norway gain entry despite all their previous planning. numerous parents pay operation freights at multiple centers in expedients of getting in nearly. This can be expensive, with operation freights ranging from$ 25 to$ 150 or further annually.

Types Of Care

There are several types of child care available to families of Young children, and there are quality pointers associated with each. In- home care is one type of arrangement that allows the child or children to remain in their home terrain. In this model of care, the provider either comes to the home or lives part- or full- time in the family's home. constantly, a relative is the person furnishing the care, and in this situation it isn't needed that a child- care license be attained. Families with low to moderate income situations frequently choose in- home care, with grandparents minding for multiple children of varying periods at one time.

Advanced- income families may have the option of hiring an au braces or a nurse to give in- home care. While there are no licensing conditions for being an au bracer or a nurse, there are interview processes and agencies that can help with this process. Generally, au dyads or babysitters give further than routine child care, frequently aiding with diurnal ménage conditioning, including running errands, shopping, doing laundry, fixing reflections, and drawing house.

The care of the child or children is the responsibility of the provider in the same way as that of a parent. Quality- of- care pointers might include a child's overall development, health, and happiness, as defined and measured by the parent and provider. There are no overall norms related to figure structure, places, and liabilities, especially in the case of relative caregivers. Payment for services is dependent on factors similar as whether the person furnishing care is entering room and board and/ or other benefits, and whether the person is a family member doing child care as a favor or as a family obligation.

Family day homes offer group care to Young children in another person's home. This is frequently a choice families make based on either the desire to keep their child in a more typical family-friendly terrain(compared to a child- care center), or on finances, since a family day home may not be as expensive as a center-grounded program. The grown-up- to- child rate may be the same, but the terrain more nearly resembles that of a family's home.

Each state has norms for family day homes and regulations regarding licensing. Unlike in- home care, which allows an unlimited number of affiliated children, family care requires licensing if children from further than one family are present. Individual countries set their own system for covering these day homes, and assessment scales are available for measuring quality of care and installations. One generally used tool is the Family Day Care Rating Scale, cooked by Thelma Harms and Richard Clifford in 1989. This standing scale assesses the quality of care related to association of space, relations between grown-ups and children(as well as grown-ups with other grown-ups, similar as other professionals or parents), schedules for Young children's conditioning, and vittles for children and grown-ups.

Child- care centers offer another option for working parents or primary caregivers of Young children. There's a great difference in child- care centers, ranging from where they're located to the freights they charge. Centers may be located in churches, at universities, in commercial settings, or in independent child- care structures. These settings may be in civic, suburban, or pastoral communities. Freights are grounded on sliding scales determined by a family's income, and literacy may be available if a family meets certain income criteria established by the agency furnishing care. Conditions vary from center to center in regard to the qualifications of staff and the program director.

Choosing Child Care

One of the topmost ways that centers differ is in their doctrines of child care. numerous child-care centers follow what's considered developmentally applicable practice for Young children, or stylish practices, as established by the associations and professionals in the field of early nonage, while some centers do not. While licensing norms are needed for child- care centers, these norms are frequently minimum, and are generally concentrated on health and safety issues rather than good- quality practices with Young children. These are only a many of the challenges a family encounters when seeking child- care services outside the home.

Families will weigh all the options for care when considering what works best for their individual child, children, or family. Every family seeking child care has its own unique set of circumstances and requirements, precedences, and enterprises regarding its children. Quality child care that's available far and wide and is standardly priced would serve a larger community, rather than being a luxury for only those who can afford it. plutocrat doesn't inescapably restate into quality care. There are several high priced centers or child- care providers that give lower than high quality services for Young children. So how does one determine quality norms of care when family situations are so unique, and when there's a similar difference in need?

pointers Of Quality Care

The significance of the first three times of life in a child's development is clear. Brain exploration from the last decade of the twentieth century shows that children are learning from the moment of birth, and that the early times give the essential structure blocks for latterly learning. It's imperative that these early guests are of high quality, and that children are given every occasion to succeed. Beforehand nonage specialists, associations, and experimenters have concentrated important attention on what constitutes quality care for babies and Young children.

Defining high quality care is grueling , however there's a general agreement among early- nonage professional associations and child- care licensing agencies regarding the orders to be included when assessing quality. There are a multitude of child- care rosters available to help families in seeking quality- care choices, as well as a multitude of provider rosters to assess the quality within their own programs.

The following issues may be considered when assessing quality of care(1) the physical setting or terrain;(2) literacy conditioning or diurnal routines;(3) relations;(4) staff, including rates of grown-ups to children, qualifications, and training;(5) health and safety issues; and(6) Mother nal involvement. Quality is addressed then as it may be measured in a child- care center, as opposed to in- home or family group child- care settings.

Physical Terrain. The physical terrain should be charming, bright, and cheerful for Young children. There should be plenty of space for children to move around, and areas should be designed to separate quiet play from active play, including in out-of-door play areas. A shy space for the number of children creates difficulties for following the routines or doesn't allow enough open space for play. Child- care regulations stipulate the minimal space permissible grounded on the number of children enrolled.

Space should be suitable for the exertion or accouterments to be used. For illustration, if children are playing in a dramatic play center, there should be ample space available to carry out the conditioning or routines of the center, similar as mock shopping with counter space for a toy register, groceries on shelves, and room to move around and pretend shop without children hitting into eachother.However, the terrain isn't duly arranged to allow children to express themselves and play safely, If space isn't available to freely move about. It's important for accouterments to be available on a child's position, to promote independence in play. A variety of literacy centers(i.e., home living, manipulative play, block area, book corner, and other age-applicable centers) offer children openings to engage in a wide range of learning openings.

diurnal conditioning and routines. Children learn to prognosticate what comes next through harmonious routines. Diurnal conditioning that allows children to be engaged in meaningful conditioning and to have some control over their terrain will foster a child's choice- timber and problem- working chops. Grown-ups should laboriously arrange the terrain to allow for independence in Young children, and conditioning should be designed to stimulate children in all areas of development, including social, emotional, physical, adaptive, cognitive, and communication disciplines.

Conditioning and routines must be applicable for the age and experimental situations of the children being watched for, and individual requirements of children should be considered in program and planning opinions. High quality child- care centers will employ grown-ups that are regardful of children's interests and probative, as well as laboriously involved in helping children resolve conflicts and problems without exercising corrective geste
strategies.

relations. Positive relations – those that indicate a healthy respect for children and grown-ups – are another index of high quality in child care.

Grown-ups in a high- quality program hear and talk to Young children and their families. They're available and responsive to the children's wants and needs, and understand the significance of development and how it impacts children at different stages. It's important that they authentically like Young children and strive to help them learn chops similar to collaborative play and to foster positive peer relations. They also understand how connections develop, and take responsibility for the part they play in making positive hookups with families of children in their care.

Staff qualifications, training, grown-up- to- child rates. State child- care licensing agencies offer minimal guidelines regarding applicable rates of child- care providers to children. public licensing associations, similar as the National Association for Education of Young Children(NAEYC), and professional associations, similar as Zero to Three, are generally more conservative in the figures they recommend as stylish practice for group size and grown-up- to- child rates, and offer good accounts for using lower figures.

High- quality connections between preceptors and Young children have been directly linked to better classroom social and thinking chops in posterior grades.

The Cost, Quality, and Outcome exploration design, conducted by the University of North Carolina at Tabernacle Hill, the University of Colorado Health lores Center, the University of California, and Yale University, produced an administrative summary in June 1999 that estimated the goods of child care on a child's after performance in academy. The overall results indicate that(1) the quality of child care is an important element for preparing Young children for academy readiness;(2) high- quality care early in life continues to have an impact on children as they move on in academy;(3) children who are traditionally considered at threat for experimental detainments due to low income or other surroundings show more positive earnings from quality child- care gests than other children; and(4) early connections with preceptors continue to impact children's social development as they move through abecedarian academy.

Programs vary in the qualifications needed for employing staff. Child- care providers have a variety of guests and training related to working with Young children. Quality pointers include personalized training or staff development for caregivers, support available for in- service training, benefits packages that support workers, CPR and first aid training conditions, formal and informal compliances of adult caregivers, and caregivers knowledgeable in child development, both typical and atypical.

Health and safety. High- quality health and safety practices bear ongoing evaluation and assessment. It's important to keep an installation or terrain clean and free of hazards. Acouterments should be routinely gutted and checked for safety. Safety preventives must be established, and programs regarding drug, hand washing, diapering or restroom training, and storing cleaning accouterments out of reach must be stuck to. High- quality programs have emergency plans in place for any medical emergency, rainfall- related exigency, or unplanned for situations. Parents should be informed and knowledgeable about these plans. Parent involvement. Parents are a child's first preceptors, and generally, parents know their children are stylish. High quality programs fit the value of including parents, who are made to feel welcome and are encouraged to be involved in whatever position they're comfortable. Parents give input to the child- care program, and they're allowed to visit whenever they choose. Positive connections between caregivers and parents are an index of quality in child care. Communication is open, regardful, and non discriminative. Parents feel comfortable participating in the information because they understand they're in cooperation with the provider. Also, parents are linked to other service providers or programs in the community that may profit their family.

A 1994 Carnegie Corporation report refers to the problems of the nation's Young children and their families as" the quiet extremity." The report states that roughly half of America's Young children start life at a disadvantage due to threat factors that include unacceptable child care. In the early twenty-first century, the well- being of numerous children is still in jeopardy due to shy child care.

The need for child care in the United States increased dramatically in the last two decades of the twentieth century – a direct result of a large increase in the chance of mothers in the pool. In 1965 only 17 percent of Mothers who had children under the age of one were in the labor force. By 1991, still, 53 percent of this group were working outside the home.

The Quality Counts 2002 report, published in Education Week, estimated that 11.9 million children, or six in ten children under the age of five, were enrolled in some form of child care during the former time. In the United States, families aren't offered expansive Mother nal leave following the birth of a child, and frequently, due to fiscal constraints, mothers or both parents must return to work soon after a new baby is born, generally within six to eight weeks. further than half of all mothers return to work within the first time after a baby's birth.

The Cost Of Care

numerous of the families who need child care also bear some fiscal backing. Child care comes in numerous forms, and there isn't a standard arrangement or figure grounded on the age of a child or a family's circumstance. The cost of care may be associated with the type of care handled, similar as child care, toddler care, preschool care, or care for children who have special requirements or those who are considered at threat due to environmental or other factors.

Child care and toddler care are generally more precious than care for a preschooler or an academy- age child, due to the number of grown-ups needed per child. In general, youngish children bear further grown-ups to give care. Rates may also vary from provider to provider based on position(pastoral or civic), character, hours of operation, population served, and conditions for preceptors. Still, there's no way to equate the quality of care a child receives with the costs associated with that care.

The charges of child care can impact a budget significantly, anyhow of who's paying for the service. A 1994 Carnegie Corporation report states that$ 120 billion to$ 240 billion are spent annually on goods and services devoted to the care and education of Young children. The average cost for care for one child can range from$ 40 to$ 200 per week, not counting operation freights, exertion freights, transportation freights, late volley freights, care for special leaves, or days a program is unrestricted and alternate care must be arranged.

The Carnegie Corporation reports farther countries that families who have inflows below$,000 annually spend 23 percent of their income on child care, while families who have inflows of around$,000 spend roughly 6 percent of their income on care. It's egregious that the lower- income family is affected more significantly when funding child care. In the United States, nearly one- quarter of the families who have children under the age of three live in poverty, and numerous are single- parent families. For these families, quality child care at an affordable cost is delicate to find.

The burden of the costs of child care is primarily the responsibility of families. Overall, families pay roughly 60 percent of child care, with the government paying 39 percent and the private sector 1 percent, according to statistics from the Quality Counts 2002 report.

goods Of Quality Child Care

There's ample exploration available in the field of early nonage education and child development that supports the significance of enriching and stimulating early guests in promoting healthy development. The first three times of life are considered pivotal, with brain development being most fleetly during this period. Parents are frequently left scrabbling to make opinions on what terrain is stylish for their child, and floundering to meet the high price of programs that claim to support these positive early experimental guests . While there are a growing number of pre – K programs for preschoolers paid for by state bones , the utmost of the costs are funded by parents. It isn't uncommon for a more elite academic preschool to bring between$,000 and$,000 annually.

exploration from the Carolina Abecedarian Project underlines the need for high- quality preschool guests for Young children from low-income surroundings. Of the 100 children studied, half attended preschool and half did not. The children studied until they reached the age of twenty- one. The children who attended preschool from immaturity to age five scored advanced on reading measures at age eight, and constantly until age twenty- one, than those children who didn't attend preschool. The summary from a 1999 cost, quality, and outgrowth study conducted by experimenters from four major universities confirms the benefits of high- quality early child care for children. In this study, high quality child care was directly linked to after academy performance and success in social development throughout the early academy times, especially for low- income children.

 Funding Options

With further emphasis on quality child- care guests coupled with the growing need for child care due to the increase in working mothers , options for funding child care are expanding, and creative ways to support the growing need are being explored. The Quality Counts 2002 report discusses how countries are seeking new sources of backing for child- care enterprise, including trying beer and cigarettes or exercising proceeds from state lotteries.

Some businesses offer workers a form of commercial child care or a flexible work plan to accommodate child- care issues. Benefits are being extended for fathers of babies, so leave isn't simply for mothers.This allows families more inflexibility in how they coordinate the first many months after a baby is born. pots are discovering that on- point child care gives workers peace of mind, allowing for further satisfaction in the work terrain and further long-term retention of workers.

In 1996 weal reform legislation was passed, furnishing nearly$ 3 billion annually in the form of block subventions to the countries for low-income families. This plutocrat is designed to give some fiscal support to single parents in the welfare- to- work program. Single parents(generally mothers) who are enrolled in a full- time work or academy program are eligible to apply for these finances to help condense their income for child- care costs.

Civil wealth finances distributed through the Child Care and Development Fund(CCDF) exceeded$ 4 billion in 2001. Also,$ 5 billion was employed for child- care backing through the Temporary backing for indigent Families program in 2000. As stated in the Quality Counts 2002 report, the subvention from the civil weal moneybags has had the biggest impact in the growth of state programs. Other programs supported through the civil government include Head Start, Title I, and the individualities with Disabilities Education Act. These programs offer fiscal backing for child care to children from low- income homes or to children who have special requirements.

Numerous countries are offering state- funded preschool programs in the early twenty-first century. While these programs aren't accessible to every child, they're targeting the population that's utmost in need of state- funded academy-grounded programs. Some countries are moving toward the conception of universal preschool. Every state provides at least some backing for kindergarten.

States struggle to erect together systems of backing that will at least support the poor populations – those who would not be suitable to gopre-school guests without subventions. Individual programs scramble to contend for available backing sources, frequently supplementing the cost of child care through subventions from agencies(similar as United

Way), private pots, or foundations. Some agencies, due to popular constraints, aren't able to offer sliding figure scales or accept state child- care instruments or literacy for children who meet income eligibility. numerous agencies work with theU.S. Department of Agriculture to land payment for children who meet income eligibility for free or reduced reflections. At best, this is a patchwork system for parents, providers, government, and unfortunately all too frequently, for the children.

and other nonprofessional positions. Preceptors are responsible for helping shape the future and enhancing a child's early development. The quality of the surroundings Young children are placed in, and the quality of the people minding for them, can impact their future.However, quality care will only be accessible to the fat, If quality is equated to bones. Because child care isn't locally accessible to all, some children won't admit the advantage of high- quality care. Families and other stakeholders that understand both the need and value of high- quality care will seek these programs for their children.